Lewis Harding

Cornwall's Pioneer Photographer

by
Philip M. Correll

The Polperro Heritage Press

LEWIS HARDING

Published by **The Polperro Heritage Press**
Polperro, Cornwall
polperro.press@polperro.org

Printed by Axion Design & Print, Bromsgrove, Worcestershire B60 3DR

ISBN 0 9530012 4 5

Foreword

Lewis Harding's grandfather was my ancestor Sir Harry Trelawny of Trelawne, near Polperro. It was through this connection I first learned of Philip Correll's talent as a meticulous researcher and serious historian who had spent many years studying the story of Lewis Harding. From his research has come this authoritative "life" written specially for the Polperro Heritage Press.

The result is this fascinating story of a most unusual life. He puts flesh on the bones of the bare facts and sets them in the living context of the world as it was in the 1800's.

This book would be worth reading simply as a mirror of the period but it is also an extraordinary narrative. Harding was born into a rather eccentric family setting and was sent away at a very early age to be looked after by relatives and then educated overseas. Between 1835 and 1846 he experienced life with the transported convicts in Australia and by the time of his return he was in need of what we would today call psychiatric help. He was extremely fortunate that the Polperro doctor was years ahead of his profession in prescribing "occupational therapy" so Lewis Harding's year studying the rooks of Trelawne (the colony still exists) was the first of its kind. He then went on to take up the new art of photography so enthusiastically that we have today a visual record of Polperro which opens a window on the hard life of a fishing village in the mid 1800's.

Lewis Harding's extraordinary story is worth telling. Philip Correll does us a favour by telling it so well.

Sir John Trelawny
Beavers Hill, Kent
November 2000

Acknowledgements

I would like to thank Professor Charles Thomas for suggesting that I research the life of Lewis Harding, and Mr Jeremy Johns for seeing this project through with his customary flair and enthusiasm. Of the many who assisted me in my researches, I would like to thank particularly, listed in alphabetical order, Fr D. Aidan Bellenger, Miss Angela Broome, Ms Chantel Celjan, the Abbé Dominique de Laforrest, Mr James Derriman, Mr H.L. Douch, Mr Ian Ferguson, Mrs Merval Hoare, Mr Dick Jolliff, Mr Andrew Lanyon, Mr Roger Penhallurick, Mme L. Rougier-Bertholet, Mrs Jill Storer, Sir John Trelawny, the late Dr Frank Turk, Sister Veronica of Sclerder, Miss Carole Vivian, Mr Pieter Wessels and Mr Trelawny Williams.

I also acknowledge with thanks permission given to me by the Royal Institution of Cornwall (R.I.C.) to use any appropriate material (i.e. text and photographs) from the Diary of John Cooke Harding and his wife Mary, and the MS copy of Jonathan Couch's *The History of Polperro*. Publication of this book has been generously assisted by a grant from the Sir Arthur Quiller Couch Memorial Fund.

I have consulted some 50 other manuscripts and books, the most important for my purpose being *Collectanea Trelawniana* (courtesy Mr Trelawny Williams); *Australasian Chronicle* (Sydney newspaper), 1842; J.V.Barry's *Alexander Maconochie of Norfolk Island*, 1958; H.N.Birt's *Benedictine Pioneers in Australia*, 1911; Mrs A.E. Bray's *Trelawny of Trelawne*, 1837; Bertha Couch's *Life of Jonathan Couch*, 1891; Mrs Merval Hoare's *Norfolk Island*, 4th edn., 1988; Andrew Lanyon's *The Rooks of Trelawne*, 1976; Eric de Maré's *Photography*, 1957; Frank Perrycoste's *Gleanings from the Records of Zephaniah Job of Polperro*, 1930; W.B. Ullathorne's *Autobiography*, 1891 and Alwyne Wheeler's transcription of the *Private Memoirs of Jonathan Couch*, 1983. Unfortunately Harding's Diary of the voyage to Australia is missing from Downside Abbey library, but extracts were published in Birt's *Benedictine Pioneers*.

Lewis Harding's photographs are reproduced on page 6, 8, 10, 14 and 21-47 as well as the covers, many by special permission of the R.I.C. The photographs on pages 5 and 13 were taken by the author.

Introduction

In the spring of 1991, when I was staying with my daughter Virginia in Sydney, Australia, I suddenly decided to fly the extra 1,000 miles to Norfolk Island, a tiny dot in the Pacific ocean to the north east. I was met at the landing field by Merval Hoare, the island's historian, and later that evening I drove alone to the deserted ruins of the old prison settlement at Kingston, by the sea. Armed with a powerful torch I found the house where Lewis Harding, the subject of this monograph, lived and worked from April 1838 to September 1842, ministering to some of the most dangerous and intractable convicts in Australasia. The clear night sky revealed the unfamiliar constellations of the southern hemisphere with absolute clarity, and I experienced in that lonely and remote place a sense of history, of the clock being turned back, and felt closer to my quarry, Lewis Harding, than any amount of reading and research could ever have achieved.

P.M.C.

Kingston, Norfolk Island today, showing the ruins of the prison by the sea. Harding's house lies just beyond the barracks in the foreground.

A collodion photograph of Polperro taken near Osprey Cottage, Lewis Harding's last home, around 1870

Man of Mystery

Lewis Harding was something of a mystery man. Since his death in 1893 at the age of 86 he has remained almost forgotten at Polperro in Cornwall where he lived for the last 30 years or so of his life, and where he produced over 300 collodion (wet plate) photographs of the village and its inhabitants, many of them of superb quality and among the earliest collodion photographs to be taken anywhere in Britain.

Two Harding treasures are stored at the Royal Institution of Cornwall in Truro. The first is a manuscript of Jonathan Couch's *The History of Polperro*, copied and expanded by his son Thomas, in which are pasted more than 200 original Harding photographs, most of them otherwise unknown. This is known as *The Polperro Book* and was apparently given to Robert Rendle when he emigrated to Australia in 1885, as a reminder perhaps of happy holidays spent at Polperro with the Couch or Rowett families, but in 1973 it was returned to Cornwall.

The second treasure is the diary of Lewis Harding's father, John Cooke Harding, continued by his wife Mary, younger daughter of Sir Harry Trelawny of Trelawne near Polperro, which covers the period 1812 to 1818. This was discovered in Brussels, where John Cooke Harding spent the last years of his life, and donated to the R.I.C. in 1989.

The diary covers an interesting period in the lives of the Hardings, and there is much information in it about their trials and tribulations at Trelawne, and later at St. Pol-de-Léon in Brittany, where they lived for many years. The Hardings were a Roman Catholic family and Lewis, their first child, was born on the 13th April 1807 at Somers Town in London, between what is now Euston station and the new British Library. Despite his privileged background, Lewis Harding's childhood was far from happy.

Lewis Harding's family links with Polperro (see Trelawny family tree on page 48)

Lewis Harding's grandfather was the Rev. Sir Harry Trelawny (1756-1834) who became the 7th baronet at the age of 16 years, inheriting Trelawne (then known as Trelawny) and numerous other estates in Cornwall. The Trelawnys were one of the most important families in Cornwall. Sir Harry and his wife Lady Anne had six children: Letitia, John, William Lewis, Hamelin, Mary (the diarist) and Jonathan. Letitia and Mary were converted to Catholicism at an early age when a French émigré priest, the Abbé Hamelin, was given sanctuary at Trelawne by Sir Harry during the French Revolution.

Trelawny House.

Two Polperro figures were of great importance to the Trelawnys and the Harding family at the turn of the 18th century. Zephaniah Job, the notorious 'smugglers' banker' and shrewd businessman whose wealth was founded on smuggling and privateering activity, managed the Trelawny family's affairs for many years, often lending Sir Harry considerable sums of money. Dr Jonathan Couch, the Polperro physician and naturalist and grandfather of Sir Arthur Quiller Couch, was to become Lewis Harding's doctor and mentor in later life.

Despite his extensive estates, Sir Harry relied on Zephaniah Job to finance him and his family over a period of 20 years and more. Long after Job's death, a local historian Frank Perrycoste was asked to look at the vast quantity of mouldering account books and correspondence at Crumplehorn Mill, Polperro, which Job had owned. He found that in 1807 Sir Harry sold Bochym, an estate situated between Helston and the Lizard, to his son William Lewis for £9,000, then a very large sum, in order to pay off his accumulated loans. However as William Lewis borrowed almost as much from Job in order to pay his father, it is hard to see that Job benefited from the transaction, apart from tidying up his book-keeping! Job trod a narrow line between maintaining a healthy banking business supported by smuggling on the one hand, and accommodating the landed gentry on the other, without causing offence to either. When he died in 1822, he left no will but nearly £8,000 in cash, which he achieved as a result of ability and hard work, besides being a beneficiary of the hard currencies of the day, brandy, rum and tobacco.

Dr Jonathan Couch (1789-1870) was a great man by any standards. A native of Polperro, he became its only doctor after qualifying in London. He was a prolific writer and his magnum opus, *History of the Fishes of the British Islands*, has not been surpassed in its field. Couch was at the same time a naturalist, antiquary and historian; he was skilled with pencil and paint brush, preached at his Wesleyan Methodist chapel, and gave fine extempore lectures. His daughter Bertha Couch described him as being "of middle height, always dressed simply in black, with frock coat, tall hat and spectacles", and added that "he was distinguished as quite  one of the old school, in that he never wore a linen collar, continuing his early fashion of a white lawn neckerchief, tied neatly in front with a small bow, with a high buttoned waistcoat."

Dr. Jonathan Couch

Several splendid photographs were taken by Lewis Harding of the good doctor, who saw generations of Polperro inhabitants into the world. Jonathan Couch was a frequent visitor at Trelawne, both as medical adviser and valued friend. His good influence on Lewis Harding is undoubted.

Lewis Harding's Early Life

It is virtually certain that Lewis was born at the Trelawnys' London house in Clarendon Square, Somers Town, and that he was baptised at the nearby Roman Catholic chapel St. Aloysius by a French priest, the Abbé Carron, who was one of many who fled France during the Revolution rather than submit to demands that the clergy become salaried officials of the state. It seems that Lewis was baptised John Aloysius Harding, and was variously called Aloysius, Louis or Lewis in his youth, and Lewis in later life.

Soon after their second child Edmund Vincent (known as E.V.) was born in 1808, John Cooke Harding and his wife Mary leased a house called Belle Vue which was a mile south of the Cistercian convent at Stapehill near Wimborne Minster in Dorset. Belle Vue was on elevated ground to the north east of Longham, but no trace of it now remains. There they were looked after by their housekeeper Miss Easterbrook, and made a number of friends amongst the local gentry and the religious. The combination of dreadful weather, which was ever present in Dorset at that time, and the loneliness of their situation, may have depressed Mary's spirits. In any event she returned to Trelawne and Dr Couch, after treating her, advised her never to return to Dorset to live. John Cooke continued at Belle Vue for a while, working at his lathe and doing odd jobs for the convent. His lack of income was obviously a problem during the early years of the family, as he apparently never followed a worthwhile occupation.

A third child Rosalie Theresa (called Theresa) was born at Trelawne in July 1812 and baptised there 'without ceremony'. At about this time Lewis, who was now five years of age, was taken to Somers Town for an indefinite period to live with his grandmother Lady Anne and his aunt Letitia, presumably as Mary was not strong enough to look after all three children. John Cooke was finally obliged to give up Belle Vue in August 1813, and returned to Trelawne in his gig, pulled by his 'poor fat mare', and accompanied by his manservant Robert Blacklock, "the terrible Robert" as Sir Harry called him. The Hardings could not afford to keep Miss Easterbrook and she was sent to Somers Town. Many of their possessions were spoiled when the vessel in which they were being transported from Poole to Cornwall overturned in the sea, but this was only the start of their troubles.

The Hardings occupied the ground floor at Trelawne, and Sir Harry and his companion Mr Rundell lived on the first floor. Mary always refers to Rundell in her diary as 'the friend', but he was not always amicable: "the friend in a horrid way tormenting and plaguing Sir H. by his unaccountable behaviour". Nevertheless Sir Harry undoubtedly discussed all manner of family problems with him. During a period of 18 months a total of 19 properties were considered for the growing Harding family, but were rejected. Either a house was unsuitable, the land poor, the freehold not available, or Sir Harry or Job, whose joint financial backing was essential, disapproved.

The predicament of the Hardings becomes clear: Sir Harry would only give them occasional financial help, it was uncertain whether or not he would ever buy a place for them, and they could not rely on the support of Job who once said they were well off at Trelawne. Matters were made worse when John Cooke's father, who made him a modest allowance, visited Trelawne and threatened to take the children away and bring them up.

Rev. Sir Harry Trelawny
From an engraving, courtesy of the National Portrait Gallery

As if all of this were not enough, Sir Harry would criticise his son-in-law John Cooke saying he was ungrateful and "had no exertion", on one occasion speaking to him harshly before all the workpeople on the estate. This caused Mary to write in her diary: "Heaven grant us patience to bear the increasing trials that every day brings us. If we can but acquire patience." But all was not gloom. There were visits to Looe Island, and to Talland Bay near Polperro where the family drank tea on the beach: "The children were in extacys". And there was often news of young Lewis from Somers Town: "A letter from my Mother enclosing one from Aloysius, his first letter. Quite pleased with it and Ed. [John Cooke] delighted. E.V. kissed it over and over again.!" Mary's sister Letitia Trelawny who taught at a school in Somers Town also wrote: "Louis can write very well & begins to learn grammar etc."

When the fortunes of the Hardings were at their lowest ebb, hope came in an unexpected way: the capture of Napoleon Bonaparte, and his exile to the island of Elba. Mary was on a visit to Lanherne convent in north Cornwall at the time and wrote: "When we came to Bodmin we saw the glorious paper that he had abdicated & the Bourbons were recalled. The Mail covered with laurels. We hurried home for our lives. Sir H was in raptures. He had white cockades for us all." These events paved the way for the prospect of living in Brittany, which had long been a favoured option for the Hardings, which Sir Harry Trelawny then supported.

On the 18th July 1814 Robert Blacklock set off, presumably for Somers Town, to bring Lewis home. On the 30th July Mary wrote in her diary, "After we had been in bed some time last night between 12 and one I heard the old study door & people walking. I called to Ed. & woke him saying perhaps Robert was come. It really was. We dressed ourselves in the dark & went down to see Louis. He took me for his aunt. I do not think him altered. He talked and did not seem much tired tho' they had walked from Torpoint & in such bad weather." Lewis, who was now seven, had not seen his family for two years.

Clarendon Square, Somers Town

12

Growing up in Brittany

Exactly one month later the Harding family and Robert Blacklock embarked on the schooner *Polperro*, the cost having been met by Sir Harry, in addition to permission being given to Mary to draw £150 a year. 'The friend' was to act as their agent. Three days later the schooner lay off the coast of Brittany at Roscoff. There Mary heard of an old chateau for sale at nearby St. Pol-de-Léon which, after negotiation with the owner at Morlaix, was purchased for six thousand livres (old French money, the equivalent at that time of about £270 sterling), and again the money was found by Sir Harry and Job. The name of this chateau or manor house, with land and gardens, stables and outbuildings, was Penenrue. Although rather run down, it was obviously a bargain.

Soon after arriving in Brittany, Lewis gave signs of disturbed behaviour, which is hardly surprising in view of the events of the previous two years or so. Attempts to educate him at home failed, so a school had to be found. Mary wrote: "Poor Louis went to school. A boy came to fetch him. He went away in a great agony. There is no help for it, he will not learn at home." Within a fortnight: "A most terrible fuss about the poor unfortunate Louis. It is now let out that almost all the boys where he is have got the itch" [scabies]. Louis was sent home and found to be unaffected, but Mary commented, "He has owned that he played with the boys 'tho he so often promised he would not. Poor Louis is our never ceasing torment."

Penenrue, St. Pol-de-Léon, Brittany

M. Moncus was then engaged as private tutor to Lewis and Vincent (E.V.). He must have been a saintly gentleman, for he persevered and Mary soon wrote: "It seems like a dream we are here. Theresa begins to say many French words & understands all that is said to her. E.V. & Louis learn with their preceptor." But that dream was soon to be shattered; Napoleon escaped from Elba and everyone at St. Pol was thrown into a state of the greatest consternation at the thought of a new reign of terror. And there was a further complication: Mary was expecting another child.

As soon as they could the family returned to Cornwall, disembarking at Polperro. Mary described in her diary how they were met by Sir Harry: "he was one of the first I saw after Mr Couch: came up to Job's with him quite overcome, but got better afterwards. We were expected & more kindly received than can be expressed." A few days later she  wrote at Trelawne: "Louis ran in saying Mr Moncus is come. We did not believe it, but it was true. Sir H. received him with the greatest kindness." Soon a school room was set up, the children in high order with their master; it amuses Sir H. to see them". But the euphoria gradually evaporated and Mary was soon to write: "I put off ugly thoughts" and later: "We have been married 9 years today and not one step advanced towards a settled menage." Soon came news of Napoleon's defeat at Waterloo, and a fortnight later he was held captive on H.M.S. *Bellerophon* in Plymouth sound.

Later a pregnant Mary wrote: "Walked around as usual with Sir H. but find it very troublesome as I am getting round and heavy. Do not think he perceives it and cannot speak of it". A few weeks later "Early in the morning was born a little girl after a dismal long labour. Theresa cannot think what the child does here & why it is come." The baby was baptised Mary Angelica Letitia (called Letitia). In March 1816 John Cooke, accompanied by M. Moncus, returned to Brittany, taking with him Lewis and Vincent. Mary and the two girls remained at Trelawne with Sir Harry, who constantly sought to dissuade his daughter from returning to Brittany for one reason or another. An ill-advised temporary return to England by John Cooke caused further tensions, but France was now stable and Sir Harry must have realised that Mary's return to Brittany was inevitable. This came about in January 1817, leaving Robert Blacklock behind as the Hardings could no longer afford to keep him.

During the following year the family were supported "in a most truly wonderful manner inconceivable to ourselves, no debts, our house much more habitable than it was, Louis going to Auray". Arrangements had in fact been made for Lewis to attend the Catholic college at St. Anne d'Auray, about 100 miles south of St. Pol and a mile or so from Auray itself. On the 6th February 1818 Mary wrote: "Louis set out for Auray, a man leading the horse with Louis seated up between the paniers containing his trousseau etc etc. The poor fellow looked back very pretty as the great doors were shutting of the court. He went away in good spirits. I feel a great consolation thinking we have sent him into the arms of St. Anne, & all the saints of our great devotion, his Patron St Louis de Gonzague etc." This is the last daily entry in the Hardings' diary.

There follow two descriptions of Lewis which are very valuable, both for their rarity and because they come from outside his family. The first is in a letter in 1818 from M. Cuenet, the Jesuit master at St. Anne d'Auray, to John Cooke: "He is a good child, and there is even something solid in him. But we think we have never seen a child as active and quick-tempered as he is. He has to be watched all the time, and still in spite of that he manages to escape, leaves his place on the bench and comes and goes to his place in class, in study; at table he moves things and overturns. If we had any number like him, it would be impossible to get on. Happily, we do not note any tendency towards vice, which, together with a basic faith we observe in him, consoles us somewhat, and gives us hope that little by little, this unceasing tumult in him will die down. I am the one who receives his confessions; he comes regularly at least every fortnight, if not every week; and we get on well enough together otherwise." Lewis was then approaching 11 years of age.

The other description is contained in Mrs Bray's novel *Trelawny of Trelawne* which she wrote following a visit to Trelawne in 1833 when Lewis was 26 years of age, his education complete: "His appearance and his manner had in them something of the foreigner: it was evident he was unaccustomed to the habits of England. But the frankness, the modesty, the kindness, and that constant attention to oblige, to consult the feelings of others, so amiable in youth, was in him so conspicuous, that it inspired esteem and regard, and rendered him a favourite with all the house."

Sir Harry Trelawny was in Italy during Mrs Bray's visit. He had become a Catholic many years earlier, and was ordained a priest in Rome in 1830. He then established a Catholic Mission at Trelawne, the priest in charge being the Rev. James Corcoran. Sir Harry died in 1834 and left life interests in his estate to the Catholic Trelawnys and John Cooke Harding, to the exclusion of those who had not embraced the Catholic faith. The will was disputed by his eldest son William Lewis who became the 8th baronet, and who afterwards said he received nothing from his father but an old pair of slippers! The death of Sir Harry, with his will disputed, may have caused financial problems for the Hardings. In any event Lewis joined the Rev. Corcoran who had now moved to Downside Abbey near Bath, as one of a select band who were to form part of Bishop John Bede Polding's Benedictine Mission to Australia. Lewis was to be a lay catechist (one who gives oral instruction in the elements of religion), and his pupils were to be convicts who had been transported to Australia, many of whom could neither read nor write.

Polding, recently appointed the first Catholic bishop of Sydney, and his party left Merseyside on the 27th March 1835 in the sailing ship *Oriental*, an old teak-built vessel which was soon put to the test in the Bay of Biscay when "a towering wave, erect as a wall" fell over it. The old East Indiaman stood it well, and thereafter the party enjoyed fine weather and fair winds. This was the start of a new life for Lewis, and he kept a diary of the voyage, which was to last nearly six months. Polding's party consisted of three priests, three sub-deacons and two catechists. Theological studies took place in Polding's cabin, and weekly social evenings were held there as well, with singing and music, helped along with a bowl of punch. Boat drill was carried out in case of attack by pirates, and Dr. Polding tended on deck some 200 different kinds of plants and flowers which he took with him.

Major penal settlements of Australia (1780-1840)
Reproduced by arrangement with the OUP, Melbourne

16

Sydney and Norfolk Island

On the 13th September 1835 the party went ashore at Sydney, cheered by the sailors who were ordered an extra glass. The appreciative Catholic population presented their bishop with a handsome carriage and pair, "expressive of their wish to maintain him in his dignity". And so Polding took up residence in a large house which the Vicar-General, the Rev. W.B. Ullathorne, had rented for him, and which alone occupied the vale of Woolloomooloo (so called by the aborigines), having an extensive garden with twenty to thirty acres of lawn in front facing the bay. This property, one half of which Polding turned into a boarding school, was a few minutes walk from St. Mary's, Sydney's Catholic cathedral, and was to be home for Lewis on and off for several years.

Polding retained one of his priests in Sydney, which contained about 6,000 Catholics, and allocated the remainder to the interior, which he divided into vast districts for this purpose. He made a point of visiting all parts of his domain, even the most distant settlements, travelling on horseback, which demanded great stamina and dedication: "I ride to Sydney tomorrow, seventy miles and I think no more of it than formerly I did of returning from Bath to Downside."

NORFOLK ISLAND
After the Naval Chart prepared for the Admiralty in 1856.

Reproduced by arrangement with the Oxford University Press, Melbourne

He had an eye for the natural beauty of Australia; sometimes he would be met at high points by horsemen, often bedecked with plumes of wattle or wisteria, to be conducted in procession into the valleys. In 1837 Harding was appointed clerk to Polding, assisting with his correspondence which had become a heavy burden. Polding was under pressure from the Governor General, Sir George Gipps, to provide a priest for Norfolk Island, but he could not spare one. However Harding offered to go, and eventually left for the island in April 1838, to prepare the ground for the priests who were to follow him. His salary was to be £100 a year, with lodgings and rations provided.

The Rev. Mr Ullathorne (later Archbishop) had visited Norfolk Island in 1834. He found the island which was of volcanic origin with its basalt columns springing from the sea, to be a botanical paradise, with its curious wild shrubs, fern trees and distinctive pines. The fauna was no less remarkable with "its beautiful pigeons, lories, parrots, parroquets, and other birds, rich and varied in plumage".

 But the captain of Ullathorne's vessel carried with him the verdicts of the court at Sydney, whereby several of the convicts were to die as a result of their part in an attempt to take possession of the island. Ullathorne prepared the men, who were kept in appalling conditions, and attended the hangings, besides ministering to many Catholics who had not seen a priest for years. These experiences left him exhausted, and despite the extreme kindnesses of the Governor Major Anderson and his wife, on his return to England he published a pamphlet exposing the unique horror of the Australasian penal settlements.

Later in 1838 Fathers John McEncroe and Henry Gregory joined Lewis Harding on the island and they all shared a bungalow, made secure from attack with heavy iron bars on the windows. The arrival of a new commandant in 1840 Capt. Alexander Maconochie R.N. signalled a change in the excessively harsh regime on the island.

A working party on Norfolk Island

When he first addressed the prisoners, 1,400 doubly-convicted felons who were accustomed to being flogged for the merest trifle and fed more like hogs than men, he wrote: "A more demoniacal assemblage could not be imagined, and almost the most formidable sight I ever beheld was the sea of faces upturned to me." Machonochie considered that the first object of all convict discipline should be the reformation of the criminal, compared with the official view that it should be a terror to evil-doers. He introduced a system whereby prisoners obtained early release for good behaviour.

Under Machonochie conditions on the island became vastly improved, to such an extent however that the relaxed discipline was viewed by some as highly dangerous, and Governor Gipps in Sydney became very concerned. At this point in June 1842 some convicts captured the brig *Governor Phillip*, a small vessel used between Sydney and the island, and lives were lost. Harding wrote against Machonochie in a letter to a friend of his in Sydney, who had it published in a newspaper there. As a result Harding was handed a letter from Machonochie: "It is further my request that you prepare to proceed to Sydney by the next brig, it appearing to me highly inexpedient, after the occurrence, that you should remain longer on this island. It gives me great pain thus to close a connection between us, in which you at one time gave me every satisfaction by your attention and assiduity in the discharge of your public duties: in which moreover, you obliged me personally by adding to them lessons given to my sons. But I really have no choice." Harding, accompanied by McEncroe sailed for Sydney on the 23rd September 1842 in the *Terror*. Harding had the support of the Church in Sydney, and the irony of the situation was that Gipps had already sent despatches to London calling for the dismissal of Machonochie. Unfortunately his revolutionary ideas were before their time, and did not receive general acceptance in prison services until a century after his death.

Capt. Alexander Maconochie
(courtesy Mr Michael Maconochie)

During his remaining time in Sydney, Harding was appointed assistant to the Rev. Mr Bourgeois, the president of the seminary, and later taught history to upwards of 40 children and students for the priesthood in the seminary, and was involved in administrative matters. One of his pupils was Frederick Milford, son of Judge Milford, who wrote in his diary: "We were principally instructed by a Mr Harding who had taken deacons orders but could not be prevailed upon to become a priest. He paid us every attention holding catechism classes and giving us good advice of all kinds. Mr Harding was a great favourite with all the family. He had a very serious illness, rheumatic fever, after we had been intimate with him for about a year [1845]: he was laid up during three months and after the fever left him he was crippled by heart affection having had a bad attack of pericarditis [inflammation of the sac surrounding the heart] during the progress of his illness. Mr Harding used to come with us at times and enjoyed our picnics very much and many of the novices of the Benedictine monastery came out for a row on holidays." Rheumatic fever would have recurred for the rest of his life, gradually weakening his heart. In October 1845 Harding wrote in the *Journal* of the Benedictines: "B. Lewis [Brother Lewis] who commences this day to write this book is weak and sickly and commends himself to the prayers of the reader."

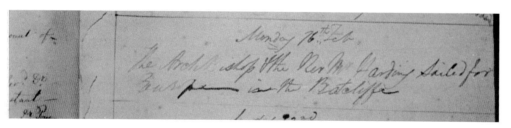

At the beginning of 1846 it became necessary for Polding, now Archbishop and in need of new recruits, to visit Rome. Harding and the Archbishop sailed for Europe in the *Ratcliffe* on the 16th February 1846. The reason for Harding's departure is not known but it was nearly 11 years since he sailed from Liverpool, he was in poor health, and the thought of returning to Trelawne and his family who were now financially secure may well have proved irresistible to him. Both his parents and the clergy had expected him to become a priest, but this was not to be.

In England Again

Dr Jonathan Couch wrote in 1850 that Harding, now aged 43, "had returned from a distant climate to Trelawny, in a very imperfect state of health", the occupational treatment prescribed by the Polperro doctor being that he should observe the actions and habits of the rooks in peace and quiet at Trelawne during the varying months of the year. In fact the Rooks Diary, which Jonathan had bound for his library and was much pleased with, was not commenced by Harding until the 28th August 1847, more than a year after he arrived back from Sydney. It was perhaps the first intensive study of any single species of bird, achieved without the use of binoculars or telescope, much of it being done from Harding's room at Trelawne. Whereas Dr Couch successfully treated him, and perhaps helped him to find a new purpose in life, he could not offer a lasting cure, and as late as 1870 his son Dr. Thomas Quiller Couch described Harding as "a great invalid".

In his analysis of Lewis's youthful erratic behaviour at the Catholic college, the late Dr. Frank Turk suggested that he may have suffered from Sydenham's Chorea (St. Vitus's dance). He commented: "It is now thought to be very closely related indeed to acute rheumatism & there seems to be a genetic background. The proximal cause of both may be a streptococcal infection or some such thing following a small injury. As with rheumatism it often leaves a malfunctioning heart & I wonder if Lewis ever suffered this in later life. It may be worth considering." The discovery of the Milford diary in Sydney confirmed Dr. Turk's brilliant diagnosis, and although he was at pains to point out that his doctorate was not a medical one, no better explanation has been found.

During Lewis Harding's absence in Australia money had been provided by the Catholic Trelawnys for the construction of a church and mission in the vicinity. This was later called Sclerder, and lies a few hundred yards to the south of Trelawne above Polperro. It was named after a tiny chapel at Kernoues in Brittany which Mary Harding visited in 1814, dedicated to Notre Dame de La Clarté, both Sclerder and Clarté meaning light.

Sclerder Abbey

For Lewis his last years at Trelawne would be a period of stability and consolidation, a preparation for the final period of his life which was to be so fruitful artistically. His brother Jonathan who was born in Brittany in 1825 married in about 1851 and lived at Porthallow House, Talland, where he farmed 150 acres. Lewis also lived in a little cottage at Talland for a time, a trial run perhaps before his final removal to Polperro.

Polperro, viewed from just above Crumplehorn around 1870.

This is a superb example of Lewis Harding's work, using light and shade. The young man with his horse and trap have been placed in the foreground to provide interest.

The Start of Photography

It was while he was still living at Trelawne that Lewis Harding became interested in photography, then in its infancy. The first indication of this is an entry in Jonathan Couch's private memoirs in October 1856: "A photograph collodion likeness is taken at Trelawny by Mr Lewis Harding, as an amusement. One a positive, holding a newspaper, one a negative, full length, holding the tusk of the African Babiroussa." Couch also added: "many portraits since."

Collodion, discovered in 1846, was made by dissolving gun-cotton in a mixture of alcohol and ether, resulting in a colourless glutinous liquid. When painted on skin it rapidly dried leaving a strong thin film, and was used as a protection for wounds. In 1851, Frederick Scott Archer used it to coat photographic glass plates. When the collodion set, the plate was immersed in a bath of silver nitrate and then placed, slightly moist, ready for instant exposure in the camera. The still moist exposed plate had to be developed immediately in a darkroom. The resultant prints had a delicacy and refinement of detail that had not been obtained before, and the new process proved to be quicker, cheaper and more certain of success. The process, known as Wet Plate, required considerable skill and patience on the part of the operator.

Dr Jonathan Couch, photographed by Harding in 1856

Unfortunately the camera was large, the tripod heavy, and Harding would have had to take with him chemicals, dishes, and a supply of glass plates, not to mention a portable dark room. Later improvements would have enabled him to prepare the plates at home and keep them moist for several days for use in the field.

Initially Harding photographed Trelawne and surrounding farms, besides taking portraits. Fortunately for us a photograph of his own family was taken in about 1856, at the front door of Trelawne. Clearly Lewis arranged the group, but someone else operated the camera. The photograph though small is clear, and is entitled 'Jonathan Harding, Mrs Harding and Lewis Harding.'

A likely interpretation of the people represented, and their approximate ages, is as follows (from left to right):

John Cooke Harding (75); Letitia Harding, his daughter (41); Mary, wife of Jonathan Harding (27); Lewis Harding (49); Ada Harding, daughter of Jonathan and Mary (4); Mary, wife of John Cooke (72); and Jonathan, younger brother of Lewis (31).

(Photograph courtesy of Trelawny Williams Esq.)

24

It is the only known photograph of Lewis, who appears to be sitting on a step, his small niece Ada (presumably) having sought out his knee. He seems to be tall, but it is impossible to be certain about this. The face of his mother Mary is indistinct; she probably moved her head during the exposure, and she partly obscures her younger son Jonathan who was described in the 1861 census as farmer and architect. It must be added that asterisks placed on the inscription to the photograph identify 'Mrs Harding' as the lady with the ringlets, not Lewis's mother. This can only indicate Jonathan's wife. Lewis and Jonathan are clearly identifiable as Lewis was much older than his brother.

By 1860 the older members of the Trelawny family had fallen to the Reaper, and soon everything was to change. Lewis's mother Mary died on the 3rd September 1857 and was buried in the little cemetery at Sclerder, to be followed by Letitia on the 6th July 1860, causing Lewis to write in an old manuscript volume of Trelawny family notes: "The writer deplores the loss of a mother, and of an Aunt who was a second mother to him," remembering his prolonged stay at Somers Town in his early years. The 1861 census shows Lewis in occupation of a cottage in Lansallos Street, Polperro, which has been identified as Ivy Cottage, postal address now Landaviddy Lane. At that time the cottage was owned by the Hitchens family, who were related by marriage to Jonathan Couch, and he may have had a hand in arranging the lease.

Ivy Cottage, Landaviddy Lane, Harding's first cottage in Polperro.
Note the temporary 'verandah' made of canvas on a frame supported by poles, an idea borrowed perhaps from Australia and intended as a protection against the weather.

In the later 1860's Harding moved a few hundred yards to Osprey Cottage, a splendid marine villa which had been built in about 1850 by Mr Halloran. It had fine views of the harbour, Peak rock and the sea, and a distinctly continental look with its steeply raked roof, and shuttered windows. This house was probably the first departure in Polperro from the traditional Cornish type of building, and it is a distinct possibility that its architect was Lewis's brother Jonathan, who had lived in Brittany for many years.

Osprey Cottage, Polperro

The view from Osprey Cottage on Talland Hill, Harding's last home, showing a schooner beyond Peak Rock

A fine example of Harding's photography dating from the 1870s. An artist, believed to be William Henry Pike (1846-1908) of Plymouth, sits opposite the Three Pilchards inn in Polperro. The cart at the harbour slip-way in the foreground carrying lime, used by farmers to improve their soil, belongs to A. R. N. Searle of Talland.

The landing of a Thrasher shark at Polperro, photographed by Lewis Harding in 1865, is causing much interest. The man at the back on the right who appears to be directing a villager to collect water to pour over the shark is probably Thomas Quiller Couch, son of Dr Jonathan Couch who had been sent the shark from Mevagissey.

A typical Harding group of fishermen, taken at Osprey Cottage using crab pots and a barrel as seats. The rugged appearance of the men contrasts with the nicely dressed little girl, or maid as they would have called her.

Seated on the left is Charles Jolliff (1808-1887), at one time landlord of the Three Pilchards Inn in Polperro. Standing next to him is his eldest son Charles (jnr), wearing an unusual pair of braces.

The fisherman seated on the right is James Curtis, married to Emily Jolliff, sister to Charles junior, so this is a family group. He is holding his daughter Kate Curtis, born in 1874, which suggests the photograph was taken around 1877.

View from the slip-way at the end of the inner harbour. The Consona boat-building yard with its odd-looking roof can be seen centre-right. This photograph is a superb study in light and shade, but the real interest is in the people and boats in the foreground. Tall hats were worn by some fishermen when they went to sea, stored in boxes after leaving harbour.

Lewis Harding's photograph of William Minards, resplendent with 'kerchief and waistcoat, is one of many portraits of Polperro inhabitants to have survived.

Minards, born at the end of the 18th century when England was still at war with France, married Susannah Cowling of Liskeard and was the village boot and shoemaker for many years, later becoming the Polperro Postmaster until his death in 1875 at the age of 77.

William and Susannah's youngest daughter, Maria Victoria, married another Polperro shoemaker or cordwainer, William Henry Curtis in 1873.

An armed Coastguard patrol at Polperro, recruited to suppress smuggling. Photographed by Lewis Harding around 1860, the men are standing on top of the lime kiln next to Harding's first cottage in Landaviddy Lane.

Polperro's reputation as a haven for smugglers led to one of the very first Preventative Service boats being stationed there in 1801. The Coastguard, orginally part of the Preventive Service, were placed under the Admiralty in 1856.

Medals worn by the men here may have included the Crimea medal and the Baltic medal.

The school lady of the day (below) with her young charges and assistants, photographed in the playground with the rock-face at the rear. This may have been Mary Rendle who had charge of the girls' school set up under the Mary Kendall charity - her assistants were Elizabeth Anne Soady and Mary Anne Bunt (Mary Rendle's niece).

The delightful group of youngsters whose footwear has been removed for better effect (above) has been arranged with imaginative use of props and interplay of light and shade, revealing Lewis Harding as a true artist. From left to right are Elizabeth Bowden, Bertha Cundy, Richard Cundy and Jack Bowden.

Dr. Jonathan Couch stands near the foot of the New Road leading down into Polperro, opened in 1849. Polperro's great man is an imposing figure in his frock coat, tall hat, pebble spectacles and large rolled umbrella, while villagers stand in groups by the roadside. It was a common saying at the time that "if Dr. Couch gave a patient up, it was no use to call anyone else in, you might just as well curl up your toes and die!"

Crumplehorn (or Killigarth) mill at the land entrance to Polperro, showing William Tucker's horse bus which journeyed to Looe and Plymouth. Harding would have positioned the subjects but could not control the horse's head, which moved during the time exposure!

Polly Colwell with pet rabbit

The Final Period at Polperro

It is ironic that so little is known of Harding during the last 30 years of his life, but his many photographs, all taken at Osprey Cottage or in the village, bear testimony to his presence there. Kate Curtis, one of several Polperro children to be photographed by Harding (see page 29), later recounted how she was often sent by her mother to see Harding at Osprey Cottage. The first time this happened Kate thought she was to have her portrait painted, but found she was to be photographed. She said Lewis would ruffle the hair of his younger sitters, for natural effect. Kate did not care for this, but clearly they were good friends, and the curious thing is that she always referred to him as 'Loysius Harding.' Children clearly liked Harding, and many of his photographs of the young people of the village have survived.

Emma and Mary Jane Oliver in seemingly spontaneous pose. The girls' dresses show fine workmanship.

Mary Jane Langmaid and Ann Elizabeth Jolliff with knitting. Children in Polperro became involved in knitting as soon as they were old enough to handle the needles.

Jane Ann Libby (on the right) with her sister Susan and baby brother Richard, born in 1865 which dates the photograph around 1866. Jane Ann, born in 1855, was one of Harding's favourite subjects.

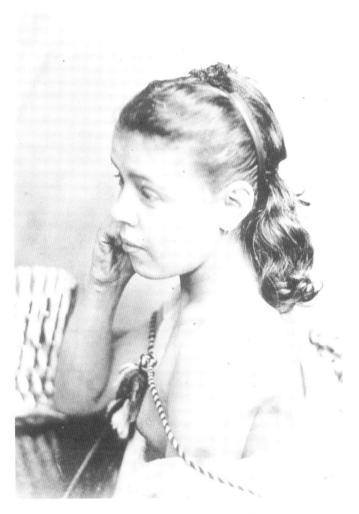

One of Harding's 'artistic' poses. The girl's rough-looking hand contrasts strangely with her face.

William Curtis and son wearing typical Polperro knitfrocks. Their distinctive patterns enabled the fishermen's wives to identify the bodies of their menfolk if they were lost at sea.

A group of important (but unidentified) visitors enjoying a picnic on Chapel cliff, above Peak Rock near Polperro. The group has been carefully arranged, with everyone looking in different directions. This works very well photographically, and is a hallmark of Harding's work (see also page 47). The servant girl in charge of the picnic hamper sits a little apart from the family, and some villagers, mostly children, look on at a respectful distance. The whole composition is an interesting social comment on the times.

Looking towards the inner harbour with St. John's Anglican chapel and Troy cottage to the left of it. The long inner quay, known as the old quay or sand quay, can be seen. This was used for landing sea-sand which was dredged from neighbouring bays and mixed with seaweed for use by farmers as fertiliser. Later the old quay was much reduced in length, the stone being used to lengthen the main quay at the entrance to the harbour.

A photograph of young village musicians, probably taken on steps off the Warren, the narrow street below Lewis Harding's home at Osprey Cottage. Note the figure behind the gate in the background.

Lewis Harding's fame as a photographer rests securely on his splendid series of more than 80 head and shoulder portraits of Polperro fishermen and other village men.

Taken at a purely pictorial level the photographs tell us all we wish to know about the sitters; they are sturdy looking individuals, which indeed they must have been to endure the hard life which was their lot, often dictated by the changing rhythm of the wind and the waves. It is unlikely however that any of them would have chosen another occupation if they had the opportunity.

In the various portraits can be seen the fishermen, John Oliver the customs man, Richard Curtis the local preacher, William Minards the boot and shoemaker, Joseph Geddye the landlord of the Three Pilchards, Edwin Oliver the youngest sitter and many others. All were part of the fabric of busy village life in Polperro which Lewis Harding so faithfully chronicled nearly 150 years ago.

These photographs, which are an artistic triumph, were probably taken over a period of years at Osprey Cottage and represent the summit of his achievment as a photographer.

Hannah Hill Hitchens Rowett, a confident well-dressed young lady signifying the importance of her family in Polperro.

This portait was taken at Osprey Cottage where dressing rooms and mirrors were available for Lewis Harding's sitters.

Hannah Rowett was born in 1850, the daughter of Richard and Hannah Rowett. The Rowetts were an important Polperro family having wide-ranging shipping and commercial interests in the 19th century. Originally from Brittany, they settled in Polperro in the 17th century and later amassed great wealth from smuggling and privateering.

Visitors to Polperro pass the Rowett Institute on their way down to the harbour from Crumplehorn.

Towards the end of his life Harding, who never married, must have lived in comfort at Osprey Cottage, having two maidservants, Anne and Helen Jolliff, to look after him. It is reasonable to assume that children were welcome there, whenever he was well enough to receive them. Then there would be conversation and laughter, and when time and light permitted the camera would be set up and likenesses taken. These would be happy occasions, with time suspended, an experience which perhaps came all too rarely to Lewis in his own childhood, all those

years earlier at the beginning of the 19th century. Lewis Harding died on the 12th October 1893 aged 86 years, the cause of death being noted as apoplexy.

In his will Lewis left his photographic apparatus, prints, photographs and photographic negatives (i.e.glass plates) to his friend and executor Joshua Brooking Rowe of Plymouth. Further research indicates they may have ended up at Plymouth or Exeter, but the air raids at both places during the last war makes their survival extremely unlikely.

Edward Puckey, John Marks and Charles Jolliff in another classic Harding group. The chain at their feet seems to symbolise the fetters of poverty, and it is all too apparent that these men had a hard life. The rope is carefully arranged to round off the group and Charles Jolliffe's braces are again on show.

A storm scene captured by Harding's camera in Polperro. Storms had devastated the harbour in 1817 and again in 1824.   Money was eventually raised to build the outer pier, finally completed in 1862.

A fine example of a large number of people of all ages co-operating in the production of a detailed and fascinating photograph. A jowter (fish buyer) wearing a tall hat is weighing fish on the market scales while the world looks on, interested no doubt in the price to be obtained for the catch. Knitting out of doors was a popular pastime because of the light; many of the cottages in Polperro had small windows and were consequently rather dark inside.

Lewis Harding was not just a photographer, he was an artist, but he worked in isolation in remote Cornwall and must have been quite unaware that he was making an important contribution to the new art form of photography, besides creating a unique pictorial record of a village and its inhabitants. And so he will always have a place in the hearts and minds of people who care about such things, and will be remembered with gratitude and affection.

TRELAWNY / HARDING FAMILY TREE

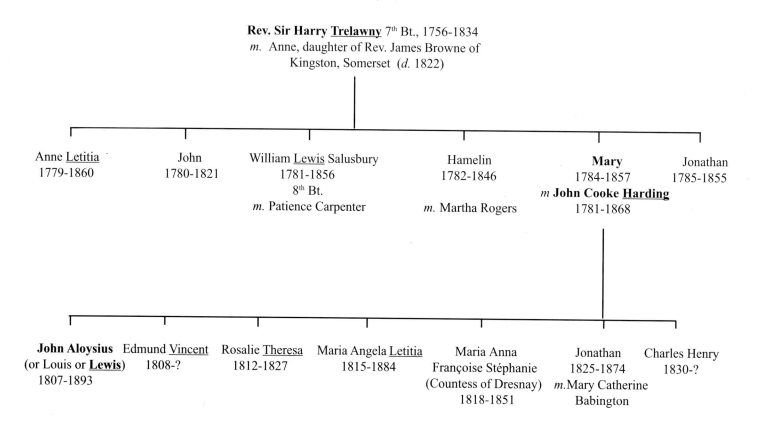

Rev. Sir Harry Trelawny 7th Bt., 1756-1834
m. Anne, daughter of Rev. James Browne of
Kingston, Somerset (*d.* 1822)

Anne Letitia
1779-1860

John
1780-1821

William Lewis Salusbury
1781-1856
8th Bt.
m. Patience Carpenter

Hamelin
1782-1846
m. Martha Rogers

Mary
1784-1857
m **John Cooke Harding**
1781-1868

Jonathan
1785-1855

John Aloysius
(or Louis or **Lewis**)
1807-1893

Edmund Vincent
1808-?

Rosalie Theresa
1812-1827

Maria Angela Letitia
1815-1884

Maria Anna
Françoise Stéphanie
(Countess of Dresnay)
1818-1851

Jonathan
1825-1874
*m.*Mary Catherine
Babington

Charles Henry
1830-?